I
STILL
DO
STUDY GUIDE

I STILL D

STUDY GUIDE

Growing Closer and Stronger
through Life's Defining Moments

DAVE HARVEY

BakerBooks
a division of Baker Publishing Group
Grand Rapids, Michigan

© 2020 by Dave Harvey

Published by Baker Books
a division of Baker Publishing Group
PO Box 6287, Grand Rapids, MI 49516-6287
www.bakerbooks.com

Printed in the United States of America

Library of Congress Cataloging-in-Publication Data
Names: Harvey, David T. (David Thomas), 1960– author. | Harvey, David T. (David Thomas), 1960– I still do.
Title: I still do study guide : growing closer and stronger through life's defining moments / Dave Harvey.
Description: Grand Rapids : Baker Books, a division of Baker Publishing Group, 2020. | Includes bibliographical references.
Identifiers: LCCN 2019035661 | ISBN 9780801094446 (paperback)
Subjects: LCSH: Harvey, David T. (David Thomas), 1960– I still do. | Marriage—Religious aspects—Christianity—Textbooks.
Classification: LCC BV835 .H36853 2020 | DDC 248.8/44—dc23
LC record available at https://lccn.loc.gov/2019035661

Portions of this text have been taken from *I Still Do*, published by Baker Books, 2020.

20   21   22   23   24   25   26   7   6   5   4   3   2   1

green press
INITIATIVE

Contents

Ending Together

STARTING T♥GETHER

.

Your Journey
through Defining Moments

> When Kimm and I were first married, I remember being baffled by the ways I behaved and the conflicts we experienced. I remember thinking, "What's happening here? Am I possessed? Or wait . . . is *she* possessed? Oh Lord, is our marriage cursed?"
>
> Over time we discovered that saying "I do" is a defining experience.
>
> *I Still Do*, p. 16

Kimm and I didn't have much preparation for marriage. In the old days, when men sported pocket handkerchiefs and women rode sidesaddle, marriage preparation seemed to be condensed into one awkward conversation with a parent before your wedding night. Nowadays, such classified information is available instantly on the web. So conversations that were once pre-wedding have been moved up, essentially, to pre-school.

As for pre-marriage training, now the awkward conversations often take place through the tag-team efforts of parents, pastors, physicians, and other counselors. Sometimes the preparation is pretty thorough. At other times it's more like a sparkler—lit just long enough for an engaged couple to note the sparkle and sizzle before it quickly sputters out. Kimm and I had premarital counseling of this variety. And honestly, I think we missed the sparkler part.

Our premarital care consisted of one session before our wedding, and that one session was focused almost exclusively upon sex. There was no discussion of the delights or complications of sex. We were simply told that we needed to talk about it. Then our well-meaning counselor handed us a crate of cassette tapes containing messages about sex in marriage and urged us to listen. With the best intentions we could muster in the frenzy of our wedding arrangements, we promptly pitched the cassettes into the boot of our car. We figured if we had any problems with sex, we'd pop the trunk. One day, nine months later, the counselor asked for his cassettes back. No problem! They were right where we left them—sitting next to the spare tire, unopened and unused.

It's unsettling to think how unprepared we were as we began marriage. The number of surprises we've encountered along the way should come as no surprise. Getting married is a defining experience. It certainly opens our eyes to things we cannot see until after we utter "I do." For one thing, marriage exposes our sin. It shows us our need for God to become man and spill his blood as our only remedy. But marriage helps us to see so much more than our sin. As Kimm and I have stacked up more and more anniversaries, we've begun to see other influences on our marriage—factors to which we were blind and matters for which we were woefully unprepared.

I'm not mentioning this to lament the past. My goal is more forward-looking and strategic. Over the years, Kimm and I have had some marriage-defining moments where we just didn't know what to do. Those experiences have often determined our progress and sometimes, quite honestly, have marked points where we've plateaued. We learned that falling in love is easy; remaining in love is something entirely different. Kimm and I have often looked back and thought, *Gee, it would have been really nice to know that sooner!*

This study guide, in conjunction with the book *I Still Do*, is intended to help you identify some of the blind spots in your marriage relationship. My goal is to talk with you about some of the defining moments—the life-defining experiences, events, and decisions—that God uses to open our eyes. God presents these sorts of moments as invitations in the life of every couple. They become the doorways to new insights or trailheads that redirect our paths. How we respond to these moments in marriage determines whether we stumble along blindly or move forward toward maturity.

Reading

Chapter 1 of *I Still Do*
Genesis 2:18–25
Ephesians 1:15–23

Reflection Questions

Here is a selection of reflection questions and activities designed to fire your affections and get you thinking deeply about the truths presented in this chapter. Grab your Bible and a pen. Write out your answers and reflections and then share them with your spouse.

1. Defining moments are experiences or seasons in life when God . . .

   • presents a decision for truth
   • requires a cost
   • offers a Christ-exalting opportunity

- grows the soul
- determines our destination

List out one moment for each of these descriptive phrases. For example, having a child that is born with a disability may be a moment that grows the soul. Moments like these often fit more than one category, but try to list five different defining moments if you can. Now think back through that list of defining moments from your life. What has God taught you through those moments?

_____

_____

_____

_____

_____

2. In the section "She Married a Harvey," I wrote about how my childhood home was a powerful shaping influence upon the way I process emotions. Often when we encounter weaknesses or personality differences in marriage, we instantly moralize them. But there are profound factors in our marriage that can't be so easily traced back to sinful desires.

What weaknesses or limitations do you have that have been shaped by your upbringing or life experiences?

_____

_____

_____

_____

3. John Calvin wrote, "Marriage is not a thing ordained by men. We know that God is the author of it, and that it is solemnized in his name. The Scripture says that it is a holy covenant, and therefore calls it divine."[1] Not only is marriage ordained by God, but all the defining moments throughout marriage are God-things as well.

Take some time to thank God for your marriage and for each of the defining moments you journaled about in question 1 above. We all have trouble understanding why God ordains some of the defining moments in our lives. He may not reveal his reasons to us in this life. However, pray that God would use these moments to grow your soul and help you to exalt Christ.

Prayer Based on Ephesians 1:18

Lord Jesus, enlighten my heart that I might see the hope you offer to those whom you have called. Open my eyes and help me to see the blind spots in my marriage—those things I'm currently unaware of. Use the time I'm devoting to this study to grant me hope in you and power for a durable marriage. Amen.

Group Discussion

Small groups reading *I Still Do* together can work through each of the reflection questions above. In addition, I'll provide a group discussion question or activity at the end of each chapter.

---

1. Quoted in John Witte Jr. and Robert M. Kingdon, *Courtship, Engagement, and Marriage* (Grand Rapids: Eerdmans, 2005), 484.

Think back through the list of defining moments you journaled about in preparation for our group discussion. As you encountered each of these moments, what blind spots did the Holy Spirit expose at each juncture? Share your reflections about how your eyes were opened to your own sin or weakness.

2

When You Discover Brokenness Is Broader Than Sin

> With a thin, oversimplified view of personhood and moral-ity, repentance—and quick repentance at that—is the go-to answer for everything that troubles us. But this doesn't work, because human brokenness is more complicated than cor-rupted hearts.
>
> *I Still Do*, p. 26

On April 30, 1943, the corpse of Major William Martin washed up on a beach in Spain. When the body was ex-amined, Nazi authorities discovered not only the typical wallet litter (license, receipts, bills, pictures, etc.) but also a letter from a general to the now-deceased Major Martin alluding, with subtle undertones, to an Allied invasion of Greece. The Nazis, justifiably suspicious of being duped, launched an extensive investigation, employing pathologists and document specialists to authenticate the body and the letter.

While this research unfolded, the Allied forces did some-thing truly remarkable, something that appeared to validate the intelligence in the letter. They began troop movements, seemingly staging for an invasion of Greece.

For the Nazi authorities, this confirmed the veracity of Major Martin's letter.

Now convinced that the Allies were planning an invasion, they redistributed their forces to fortify the Balkan Peninsula, pulling troops away from Sicily . . . just as the Allies had hoped.

The whole thing was a ruse.

The Nazi army had been fooled, the unwitting victims of an elaborate web of disinformation known as Operation Mincemeat. The military buildup near Greece had been a tactical ploy, complete with fake troops and inflatable plastic tanks. "Major Martin" was a real corpse, but the letter and identity were all fake, planted on the body as a diversion. And how did the Allies fool the Nazi experts? Well, they created a backstory for Major Martin that was so thorough, it included running his obituary in a London newspaper.

The Allied invasion site was actually Sicily, five hundred miles away from Greece and the very place the Germans had withdrawn their troops from to fortify Greece. This seduction of the Nazis away from Sicily to Greece has been called the most spectacular single episode in the history of deception.

The story is a reminder for me that life is often more complex than it first appears. As J. I. Packer writes, "The more complex the object, the more complex the knowing of it."[1] Here's the truth: the simplest explanation of events isn't always the best one. That applies whether we're talking about understanding the art of warfare or understanding something that's infinitely more complex—your spouse. Don't misunderstand me; I'm not saying that your spouse is your enemy. But I am saying that you should study your spouse with the same intensity that a military leader studies the tactics of

1. J. I. Packer, *Knowing God*, 20th anniversary ed. (Downers Grove, IL: InterVarsity, 1993), 35.

opposing forces in wartime. In marriage, God invites us to fully know another human being.

If your pattern of studying your spouse involves reducing and oversimplifying your spouse's life and motivation, you're likely being duped by the enemy (2 Cor. 2:11). Moreover, you miss the opportunity to truly care for the complex gift God has given you in your spouse. To skillfully love and care for them as a *whole* person, you must see beyond the surface to the desires of their heart and also consider their physical, relational, and family background— realities that have shaped who they are.

Reading

Chapter 2 of *I Still Do*
Genesis 37:1–36; 50:15–21
James 4:1–10

Reflection Questions

Here is a selection of reflection questions and activities designed to fire your affections and get you thinking deeply about the truths presented in this chapter. Grab your Bible and a pen.

Saying sin is our biggest problem doesn't mean sin is our only problem. Answer the following questions about the first three of the nested circles described in chapter 2. Write out your answers and reflections and then share them with your spouse.

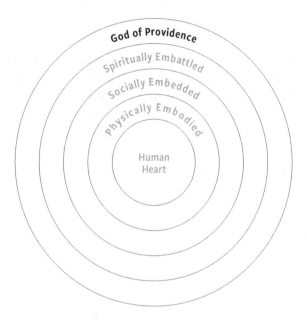

1. *The Human Heart.* James tells us that outward sins like anger and quarrels are rooted in the evil desires that battle within us (James 4:1). What sinful behaviors—anger, lust, jealousy, or greed—do you regularly battle? What do these behaviors say about the misplaced or unfulfilled desires of your heart? Confess this to your spouse. Then humble yourself before the Lord and ask him to order your desires in accordance with his will.

_____

_____

_____

_____

_____

2. *Physically Embodied.* How are your aging body and physical limitations impacting the way you interact with your spouse? List out factors that impact you daily, such as forgetfulness, joint aches, menopause, or depression. Does recognizing such bodily limitations in yourself give you empathy for your spouse when he or she faces similar limitations? Why or why not?

_____

_____

_____

_____

3. *Socially Embedded.* Your family of origin has a strong influence on the person you are today (Num. 14:18). It does not define you (Phil. 3:13–14), but it does impact you in ways you may not be aware of. Take a look at the list of family background questions in the chart below. Think through them carefully.

What one or two insights are you becoming aware of that help you to make sense of how your family of origin (and perhaps that of your spouse) shapes your marriage today?

_____

_____

_____

_____

FAMILY BACKGROUND QUESTIONS

- Describe each member of your family of origin with three adjectives and identify their relationship to you (parent, caregiver, grandparent, sibling, etc.).
- Describe your parents' or caretakers' marriage(s) as well as your grandparents' marriage(s).
- How were conflict, anger, and tensions handled in your extended family over two or three generations?
- Were there any family secrets? (For example, an unwed pregnancy, incest, mental illness, or financial scandal.)
- What was considered "success" in your family?
- How did ethnicity or race shape you and your family?
- How would you describe the relationships between family members? (For example, conflicted, detached, codependent, abusive, etc.)
- Were there any heroes in the family? Any villains or favorites? Why were these individuals singled out in this way?
- What generational patterns or themes do you recognize? (For example, addictions, affairs, abuse, divorce, mental illness, abortions, children born out of wedlock, etc.)
- What traumatic losses has your family experienced? (For example, sudden death, prolonged illness, disability, stillbirth/miscarriage, bankruptcy, divorce, etc.)

Adapted from Peter Scazzero, *The Emotionally Healthy Leader: How Transforming Your Inner Life Will Deeply Transform Your Church, Team, and the World* (Grand Rapids: Zondervan, 2015), 74–75.

Prayer Based on Galatians 5:16-26

Father, help me to walk in step with your Spirit. Make me aware of the ways I'm easily deceived, and grant me desires that are aligned with your will so that I may know my spouse as a whole person. As I know my spouse more deeply, allow our marriage to endure and bear spiritual fruit. Amen.

Group Discussion

Small groups reading *I Still Do* together can work through each of the reflection questions above. In addition, here is one more group discussion question for this chapter.

Joseph was able to look back at the many traumatic events of his life—including the ways he was sinned against by his brothers—and see God's purposes (Gen. 50:20). The family background questions above are designed to help you become more aware of patterns of brokenness in your family history. But while people may have done or intended evil, God was working for good. Share now with the group about how you see God's providential hand at work in your family history.

DEFINING MOMENT #2:

The Moment of Blame

> Hiding in darkness is a chronic problem. And it gets worse as we age. Not only do we have a natural bent toward avoiding blame but, barring a growing affection for God, our willingness to accept responsibility weakens as we grow older.
>
> *I Still Do*, p. 51

In my scribblings as an author, I've written a bit about sin and its effects. If you read my early stuff, like *When Sinners Say "I Do,"* you may think I had a knack for finding sin needles in every haystack of life. That was true, undoubtedly, of my younger years, when I often reduced complex issues to two shades—black or white. But age, experience, repentance, and a growing awareness of God's heart have led me to what I pray is a more circumspect view of humanity.

These days I'm much more cautious about quickly assigning sinful categories or motivations to people. After all, people are complex. "Sin or no sin?" may appear to simplify leadership decisions, but it ultimately creates a greater mess. We can't reduce all human behavior to righteousness and evil. There are other factors involved. As we explored in the last chapter, there's a complex interplay between body, soul, environment, family history, and even the enemy. To accurately discern motives, we sometimes need good pastors *and* good physicians.

In a similar way, I think we tend to distill the narrative in Genesis 3 to an account that's merely about the origins of sin and brokenness. That's oversimplified too. Genesis 3:1–13 is really a broader tutorial on the character, nature, and tendencies of imperfect people. It's about the diabolical design of how sin operates within humans.

If Genesis were the *Star Wars* saga, chapter 3 would be like the stolen architectural plans to the Death Star. It reveals specific ways we're vulnerable to attack and destruction. It diagrams for us the particular places our enemies—the world, the flesh, and the devil—are most likely to attack. One aspect of our brokenness—an exhaust port that leads to our core reactor (keeping with the *Star Wars* analogy)—is the matter of our agency or moral responsibility.

Part of original sin's fiber—part of its character—is the tendency to deflect agency from us and ascribe our sinful decisions to others. When Adam blamed the woman, he shifted his God-ascribed moral responsibility away from himself and tagged her: "The woman you put here with me—*she* gave me some fruit from the tree" (Gen. 3:12 NIV, emphasis added). This seemingly clever evasion on the man's part revealed a potent desire embedded in all sin. Sin seeks to shift our status before God and man from being morally responsible (and therefore culpable) to being the victim of other people's decisions. The ultimate insanity is that we convince ourselves we are also victims of God's decisions. After all, it was "the woman *you* put here with me" who delivered the fruit.

When sin arrives for work, it clocks in early and works overtime. When sin speaks, it supplies our hearts with a passive voice. "Me?" Adam says, "I'm just a bundle of goodness enjoying the garden—walking and talking with God, spreading his glory. The bad things are happening *to* me. It's that woman, Lord. *She* gave it to me!" In Adam's mind, sin was done *to* him, not *by* him. Moral agency was swapped for self-pardon. Under the sway of sin, his self-understanding had only one category—sinned against.

When sin knocks, everyone except us is guilty. Even God!

What about you? Have you ever noticed that when we tell our own story, including some of the trials and pains, we're rarely positioned in the story as a sinner with junk? More often we see others as actors on the stage, committing sins against us or omitting things they should have done for us.

Reading

Chapter 3 of *I Still Do*
Genesis 3:1–13
Philippians 2:1–11

Reflection Questions

Here is a selection of reflection questions and activities designed to fire your affections and get you thinking deeply about the truths presented in this chapter. Grab your Bible and a pen.

In the chapter I wrote about how humility helps us by instilling proper self-suspicion and establishing our daily need for God's amazing grace. Are you growing in humility? Take time to journal through these questions from the "at-home" humility test that I outlined in chapter 3. Write out your answers and reflections. Answer honestly, and share them with your spouse when you're done.

1. *How do I respond when my spouse corrects me?* Do you bristle at correction? Or do you consider what's being said and humbly receive the reproof?

_____

_____

_____

_____

_____

2. *How do I respond when I think my spouse has sinned against me?* Do you tend to retaliate or give yourself special permission to be angry and cynical toward your spouse when they've sinned? Or do you remember how Christ responded even when we acted as his enemies (Rom. 5:10)?

_____

_____

_____

_____

3. *How do I describe my largest internal obstacles?* Do you tend to use words that acknowledge your personal responsibility, or do you tend to shift the blame? When you think about the problems in your marriage, do you start with blaming your spouse? Or are you willing to humbly accept the blame when you know you are wrong?

_____

_____

_____

_____

4. *How do I respond when I become aware of my own failures and weaknesses?* Do you tend to believe the lie that you are a victim of fate? Do you rely on yourself, proudly protecting the illusion of your perfection or trying to atone for your sin by doing good works? Or do you flee to the Savior? Do you own your failure and your sin before a holy and loving God as well as before your spouse? Have you found that Christ is perfectly sufficient to meet you exactly where you are struggling?

5. *Am I growing more amazed by grace?* Are you able to see your daily need for Christ's love and gospel renewal? Are you amazed at Christ's sufficiency to meet you exactly where you're hurting and struggling? Are you growing in awareness of how the gospel applies to your specific sins? Are you moving toward your spouse to confess these sins? Are you expressing gratitude to God for his astounding pardon and power?

WHAT DOES MY SPOUSE THINK ABOUT MY HUMILITY?

I've found the at-home humility test questions to be helpful as a self-assessment. But often self-assessments—particularly self-assessments of our humility—are not as accurate as the assessments of others. This ten-question quiz allows your spouse to gauge your ability to humbly engage and receive his or her influence.

Ask your spouse to take the following quiz, circling T for true and F for false.

My spouse . . .

1. **T F** is really interested in my point of view.
2. **T F** communicates respectfully even when we disagree.
3. **T F** wants me to feel that what I say really counts.
4. **T F** doesn't reject my opinions out of hand.
5. **T F** believes that I'm more important than winning the argument.
6. **T F** always consults me before making major decisions.
7. **T F** can challenge me with grace and care in areas where I need to grow.
8. **T F** can often find something to agree with in my position.
9. **T F** usually thinks I have good ideas and I can help at problem-solving.
10. **T F** sees the importance of serving each other in our marriage.

Scoring: Score one point for each true answer.

The higher your score, the more your spouse receives you as a person who is willing to receive their influence, and that is a mark of humility. If your score is lower (below 5), work back through the questions. Then spend some time meditating on Philippians 2:1–11 as well as James 4:1–10. Ask the Holy Spirit to reveal specific ways that you've acted in arrogance and pride. Confess these ways to God and your spouse.

Prayer Based on James 4:1–10

Father, your Word tells me that fights and quarrels cannot be blamed on others. They come from the desires that wage within me. I confess my pride and selfish ambition. Grant me deep sadness and contrition over my sin. Help me to see it as a grievous sin against you. Humble me by reminding me how Christ humbled himself. Draw near to me, Father, by your grace, so that I may only be lifted up in becoming a servant like Jesus. Amen.

Group Discussion

Small groups reading *I Still Do* together can work through each of the reflection questions above. In addition, here is one more group discussion activity for this chapter.

WHAT THE CROSS TELLS US ABOUT CRITICISM

In the chapter I wrote about clinging to Christ when you become aware of your weaknesses and failures. Review these twin truths that the cross teaches us about criticism and answer the questions below in a journal. Then review the answers in your study group.

First, the cross shows us that God sees us as sinners. There is no escaping the truth: "No one is righteous—not even one" (Rom. 3:10 NLT). The cross doesn't merely criticize or judge us; it condemns us for not doing *everything* written in God's law (Gal. 3:10).

- No one can criticize you more than the cross already has. When your spouse criticizes you, do you remember that

God is your first critic? Do you agree with God's criticism of you?

- Do you feel the force of God's criticism? Do you appreciate the thoroughness of his judgment?
- How well do you take advice? When your spouse criticizes you, do you remember God's judgment of you and assume there is at least a kernel of truth in the critique? Or are you quick to reject the content of his or her criticism?

Second, at the cross we see how God justifies us. Through the sacrificial love of Jesus, God justifies ungodly people (Rom. 3:21–26). The cross reminds us that the Son of God loved us and gave himself for us (Gal. 2:20).

- Through Christ, the most devastating criticism becomes the finest mercy (Ps. 141:5). Knowing that God intends mercy through the rebukes we receive, do you respond to your spouse's criticism—even mistaken or hostile criticism—without bitterness, defensiveness, or blame shifting?
- Do you pout when you're criticized? Do you harbor anger against the person who criticizes you? Do you immediately seek to defend yourself, hauling out your righteous acts and personal options?
- Do you remember that what justifies you is not being right but being made right through God's justifying verdict? How does meditating on Christ's love change your tone and response to your spouse?

Adapted from Alfred J. Poirier, "The Cross and Criticism," *The Journal of Biblical Counseling* 17, no. 3 (Spring 1999): 16–20.

DEFINING MOMENT #3:

The Moment of Weakness

Paul rolls out a paradox—an apparent contradiction—that seems utterly nonsensical at first blush. Paul makes weakness his defense. His argument unfolds this way: "You think I'm weak? Well, I've got wonderful news for you. I'm weaker than you could ever imagine. I'm gloriously weak! In fact, I want to *boast* about my weakness."

I Still Do, p. 61

Kimm is not a *Lord of the Rings* fan. Not even a little. She thinks the wizard Gandalf is moody and constantly irritated. And honestly, I think that's pretty accurate. I told her that he's practically holding all of Middle-Earth together, but she said that watching him was too much like raising teenagers.

There's a scene in the first *Lord of the Rings* movie where Gandalf is discussing the future of Middle-Earth with Elrond, the Elven lord of Rivendell. In the dialogue, Elrond says something insightful about the race of Men in Middle-Earth that holds true both in his fictional world and in the universe where we reside.

ELROND: The time of the Elves is over. My people are leaving these shores. Who will you look to when we've gone? The Dwarves? They toil away in caverns, seeking riches. They care nothing for the troubles of others.

GANDALF: It is in Men that we must place our hope.

ELROND: Men? Men are weak. . . . I was there the day the strength of Men failed.[1]

Elrond is right. It's true that the human race is weak. We've fallen. And the strength of humanity still fails in this day. We are the oversleepers, the bill-forgetters, the "Oh-Lord-what's-that-smell" people.

And yet Paul boasts "all the more gladly" in his weakness (2 Cor. 12:9 NIV). You see, our weakness shows us that we are not God and then it pushes us into desperate dependence upon him. Ultimately, God meets us in our weakness. In our failings and fallings, he continues to show us a grace we did not earn and could never deserve. This should humble us and reinforce our need for Jesus each and every day.

God also uses our thorns to connect us to his strength. Weakness is the place where we meet God in our inability and discover his remarkable power. Kimm and I moved through our first decade not really understanding this lesson. I suppose we had thorns in the first decade, but we never really saw them as gifts given to us by Jesus to accomplish something eternal. Part of me hoped that my sense of weakness would diminish as my experience of marriage grew. And sure, knowing one another better and sharing love and pain provided a strong foundation to build many memories and

---

1. "The Fate of the Ring," *The Lord of the Rings: The Fellowship of the Ring*, directed by Peter Jackson (New Line Home Entertainment, 2001), DVD.

weather some big storms. But as we matured in marriage, God honored us by sending thorns our way.

I find it amazing and instructive that God gave Paul a thorn right after the apostle's magnificent experience in the third heaven. Sometimes good things deliver us to hard places. Our heart rejoices in the experience of the good rather than in the Giver of the good. As a result, we need to learn the humility and dependence that weakness teaches. In an act of love, God takes the things we would be tempted to glory in and converts them into places where we desperately need him.

Reading

Chapter 4 of *I Still Do*
2 Corinthians 12:1–21
Hebrews 4:14–5:10

Reflection Questions

Here is a selection of reflection questions and activities designed to fire your affections and get you thinking deeply about the truths presented in this chapter. Grab your Bible and a pen. Write out your answers and reflections and then share them with your spouse.

1. Weakness is a reality in marriage because we are not God. We are the creatures, not the Creator. But it's not merely that we're limited as creatures. We are also fallen. In the chapter I wrote about two types of weakness—*deadly inability* and *daily inability*. Describe where you have seen these two at work in your life.

First, what are the besetting sins (deadly inabilities) that seem to continually raise their ugly heads in your heart and behavior? Write them down.

When we struggle with recurring sins, we should experience this as a reminder that we cannot save ourselves. We desperately need Jesus. Confess this truth to him right now.

Second, what areas of limitation, vulnerability, or frailty (daily inabilities) have you experienced this week? Write them down. Kimm has a bad knee; I travel with a back-pillow, compliments of lower-back arthritis. How might your own physical, emotional, or mental frailties be a channel for the movement of God?

---

2. God uses our thorns to make us dependent upon him.
   How have the weaknesses and thorns in your life led you
   to greater trust in God? What are some practical ways you
   demonstrate that trust?

_____

_____

_____

_____

_____

3. God uses our thorns to show us that the other things we
   rely upon cannot ultimately satisfy. How has your weakness revealed your entitlement or your dependence on false
   hopes?

_____

_____

_____

_____

Prayer Based on Philippians 4:12–13 and Martin Luther's Midday Prayer

*Father, help me to learn the secret of being content. Although
the events of my life have not always transpired in line with
my hopes and expectations, I place my hope in you, no matter the circumstances. Help me to embrace both poverty and
wealth, sickness and well-being, through Christ who gives
me strength. Amen.*

Group Discussion

Small groups reading *I Still Do* together can work through each of the reflection questions above. In addition, here is one more group discussion question for this chapter.

We find access to God's power through the One who understands our thorns. Jesus knows our weakness. He was tempted in every way that we are, yet without sin. Consider this quote from Raymond Brown and share your reflections with the group.

> No one on earth, before or since, has ever been brought through such spiritual desolation and human anguish. For this reason, [Jesus] can help us in our moments of temptation. He is aware of our needs because he has experienced to the full the pressures and testings of life in this godless world.[2]

2. Raymond Brown, *The Message of Hebrews*, The Bible Speaks Today (Downers Grove, IL: InterVarsity, 1982), 92.

STICKING T♥GETHER

DEFINING MOMENT #4:

When You Realize Family Can't Replace Church

> Right now family serves an earthly purpose. But the day will come when it will be transformed into a glorious experience that is multiplied and magnified by the larger family to which we are united.
>
> *I Still Do*, p. 87

John Piper once observed, "The church of Jesus Christ is the most important institution in the world. The assembly of the redeemed, the company of the saints, the children of God are more significant in world history than any other group, organization, or nation."[1] But what happens when married couples begin to think that family is more important than the church?

Okay, I'm going to say it now, and I want you to think about it. Are you ready?

The whole idea of family, in the way we experience it on earth, is only temporary. There is a day coming when the concept of

---

1. John Piper, "The Cosmic Church," sermon preached on March 22, 1981, accessed online at https://www.desiringgod.org/messages/the-cosmic-church.

family will be swept up into a more glorious and satisfying arrangement. Don't let that make you nervous. What awaits us is far more magnificent.

One day the Sadducees tried to trick Jesus with a question about heaven. Jesus answered, "In the resurrection they neither marry nor are given in marriage, but are like angels in heaven" (Matt. 22:30). Jesus is not saying that because marriage isn't eternal, it's time to toss it on the trash heap. No, he's telling us that something even better awaits. In heaven there will be one glorious marriage between Christ and his bride, and that marriage will satisfy and complete every desire we've had for marriage on this earth.

In fact, the eternal marriage between Christ and the church is the very point for which marriage in this life exists. Marriage on earth is a picture of that eternal reality. It mirrors a higher purpose. Paul explains, "'Therefore a man shall leave his father and mother and hold fast to his wife, and the two shall become one flesh.' This mystery is profound, and I am saying that it refers to Christ and the church" (Eph. 5:31–32).

In glory, you will experience delight that far outweighs what you've experienced here and now. If your spouse is there too, it's hardly a stretch to think you'll experience heavenly delight in Christ along with your spouse—the one you've delighted in most in this life. But you won't delight in your spouse because your earthly roles are enduring. You'll find delight in your believing spouse because you've met the One to whom they pointed you in this life.

In Pittsburgh, where I grew up, there is a beloved amusement park called Kennywood. Back in the day, posted all around the 'Burgh were yellow Kennywood signs pointing in the direction of what we believed to be the ultimate amusement experience—cotton candy, caramel apples, delicious treats. Oh, and did I mention the roller coaster that would stop your heart and expel the candy you gobbled up straight onto the coaster tracks? Throwing up at Kennywood was a rite of passage, something to boast about in English class on Monday.

The Kennywood signs around the 'Burgh pointed people in the direction of our deep desires for amusement park pleasure. But the signs were not the reality. Just imagine the poor kid sitting under a Kennywood sign thinking that's all there was to this wondrous place. He'd be pretty misguided, wouldn't you say? The sign, of course, served another purpose. It pointed forward to something else—something that would fill that child with unexpected joys.

When sinners say "I do" in this life, they become signposts pointing to the relationship with the Bridegroom, Jesus Christ. Once we arrive in heaven, the signs will no longer be necessary. They will be caught up into something more amazing than any amusement park—the marriage of Christ and the church.

What's true of marriage is true of family. Earthly families will be swept up into a greater reality—the body of Christ. This is not to say our believing family members will become strangers in the new earth. "Do I know you? You look vaguely familiar. Were we friends on Facebook?" Rather, as Rob Plummer writes, "If our children stand beside us in eternity, it will not be as our children but as our blood-redeemed brothers and sisters."[2]

It's not so much that we lose our old family but that we gain a new family—a larger eternal one. Right now family serves an earthly purpose. But the day will come when it will be transformed into a glorious experience that is multiplied and magnified by the larger family to which we are united. As Randy Alcorn has said, "God usually doesn't replace his original creation, but when he does, he replaces it with something that is far better, never worse."[3]

2. Robert L. Plummer, "Bring Them Up in the Discipline and Instruction of the Lord: Family Discipleship among the First Christians," in *Trained in the Fear of God: Family Ministry in Theological, Historical, and Practical Perspective*, ed. Randy Stinson and Timothy Paul Jones (Grand Rapids: Kregel, 2011), 50.
3. Randy Alcorn, *Heaven* (Wheaton: Tyndale, 2004), 337.

Reading

Chapter 5 of *I Still Do*
Ephesians 1:22–23
1 Timothy 3:14–16

Reflection Questions

Here is a selection of reflection questions and activities designed to fire your affections and get you thinking deeply about the truths presented in this chapter. Grab your Bible and a pen. Write out your answers and reflections and then share them with your spouse.

1. The Bible makes clear that parents are to be the primary disciple-makers for their children (Deut. 6:1–9; Ps. 78:1–8). The New Testament world would have agreed with ours that biological and adoptive family relationships are vitally important in this life. But Jesus also makes abundantly clear that our family relationships must not be our first priority (Matt. 10:34–39; 12:48–50; Luke 14:26). Christians today typically emphasize one of these truths or the other. What is/was your tendency as a parent?

   _____

   _____

   _____

   _____

   Do you have a "drop-off" mentality—entrusting church leaders or programming with the primary responsibility for teaching your children the Bible? Or do you over-prioritize your family, like the father who makes his own patriarchal leadership into an idol?

_____

_____

_____

_____

2. Many people have horrible experiences with their families. If the whole concept of family calls to mind brokenness and pain, memories that elicit deep shame, or something from which you had to flee, please know that what God is preparing for you is not simply a family reboot. Rather, it's what family should have been all along—only more glorious. Your next home will be led by a perfect Father and occupied by new brothers and sisters who have shed the scales of sin.

What truths about our eternal family from the chapter provide you with the most comfort? Why do these truths comfort you? Write these reasons in your journal.

_____

_____

_____

_____

3. The Western church loves private, personal stuff. We have *personal* Bible study, *personal* evangelism, and *personal* prayer—all designed to enhance our *personal* relationship

with Christ. None of this is wrong. In fact, much of it is quite helpful. But our personal relationship with Christ is only a slice of the Christian experience.

What regular disciplines could help you to cultivate a more corporate experience of Christ? How, for instance, are you doing with meeting with God's people? Do you see it as essential to the future of your marriage? Do you make being with the people of God a priority?

_____

_____

_____

_____

_____

Prayer Based on 1 Timothy 3:14–16

Jesus Christ, you appeared in the flesh. At your resurrection you were vindicated by the Spirit. You ascended and were welcomed into heaven by the angels. Your gospel message has been preached throughout the whole world. Your church is the pillar and foundation of the truth. You are in first place—preeminent. Let your priorities be the priorities of my family. Amen.

Group Discussion

Small groups reading *I Still Do* together can work through each of the reflection questions above. In addition, here is one more group discussion question for this chapter.

In the chapter I mentioned how we can let our kids' extracurricular activities take priority over being with God's people. I've noticed that involvement in sports takes a particular toll on a family's commitment to gather with the church. Weekend games and practices are more and more common today. And for gifted athletes who participate in travel ball, weekend games take a family away from their hometown and church multiple times each season.

Have you considered what the choices we make about athletics communicate to our kids about what's most important in our lives? What extracurricular activities tempt your family to be away from the church community? Confess your temptation to your spouse and to your small group.

6

DEFINING MOMENT #5:

When Your Spouse Suffers

> Blessed be the God and Father of our Lord Jesus Christ, the
> Father of mercies and God of all comfort, who comforts us
> in all our affliction, so that we may be able to comfort those
> who are in any affliction, with the comfort with which we
> ourselves are comforted by God.
>
> 2 Corinthians 1:3–4

People are diverse and life is complex. Our stories are like snowflakes—no two exactly alike. You may feel like you can't relate to your suffering spouse—like he or she needs someone else who has experienced the same sufferings. But God has been at work in you to make your story more relevant and powerful for your spouse than you might think. Believe this when you're seeking to help them. Your story doesn't need to replicate your spouse's experience of suffering; you just need to empathize with their affliction. It's not about commonality but sympathy. In other words, you don't have to have an experience that is an exact copy of theirs to be able to help. The connecting point for true help is not the exact similarities between your struggles but the common human responses those struggles trigger.

Jesus, the perfect high priest who can sympathize with our weaknesses (Heb. 4:15), did not share every human's experience. His sympathy comes from his common experience of being tempted. Touching humanity in this one area gave him the ability to sympathize with us in all areas. Because he was tempted like we are, yet without sin, Jesus now speaks our language and understands our pain. You may have never lost a child through a miscarriage, but perhaps you have grieved the loss of someone close to you. You can't reproduce the exact dimensions of another person's grief, but you are familiar with the category of loss, the places the heart goes, the way one might be tempted, the manner in which God may be wrongfully charged, the why questions that flog the soul. You have experienced loss and understand the temptations that grief carries with it. You have a vocabulary for pain, so you can speak the language of the sufferer and sympathize with the difficulty within their soul.

When your spouse in particular is suffering, where is God in their story? How do they see his role? How do you see it? Is he absent from your conversations about the pain? Maybe your spouse sees God as being present but punishing him or her through this affliction. Is God's providence a present comfort to them or is it more like a dull haze on a distant shore? In these moments we shouldn't be put off by our spouse's incorrect theology or start an argument with them. Rather, it's more important to cast a vision for them of God's love and care.

As Paul comforted the Corinthians, he did so from a place of experience. He was able to draw upon the comfort he'd already received from God. It may surprise you, but just as God prepared Paul, he has prepared you for this moment. Remember Paul's words: God sometimes *gives us* affliction to supply comfort and compassion to other people. Take that in. God is so serious about helping you care for your spouse that he arranged some past experience of pain or affliction for you to draw upon.

Now, don't misunderstand me. When your spouse is suffering, James 1:19 is never more relevant: "Let every person be quick to hear, slow to speak, slow to anger." But after you've listened well, don't be afraid to wade in and speak words of compassion and care. Draw from the ways God has walked with you through your own griefs.

Reading

Chapter 6 of *I Still Do*
Romans 8:28–30
2 Corinthians 1:3–11

Reflection Questions

Here is a selection of reflection questions and activities designed to fire your affections and get you thinking deeply about the truths presented in this chapter. Grab your Bible and a pen. Write out your answers and reflections and then share them with your spouse.

1. Describe what it looks like for a spouse to be purposefully present in suffering. What are the kinds of things that keep us from being present?

2. When suffering comes, which of these three fallen heroes do you most resemble? Do you become passive like Adam?

Do you become cynical like Job's wife? Or do you become self-protective like Abraham?

3. In the chapter I described some of my less-than-stellar moments of loving Kimm when she is suffering. With which of these Daves do you most identify?

Dave the Diligent—never checked out of the office enough to be fully present.

Dave the Martyr—parlaying his wife's afflictions into a celebration of himself.

Dave at a Safe Distance—the Dave who asks, "How far can germs jump?"

"Won't Let You Tell Your Story" Dave—his spouse's suffering triggers some similar story from his personal history.

"Draw Up the Will" Dave—his care is clouded with his worries over each potential danger.

4. Review this quote from the chapter, spend some time journaling your reflections, and then share them with your spouse:

> God could have resolved the problem of sin without addressing the effects of sin and suffering that touch our daily lives. But he's too good for that. He comforts us *in* our affliction with a comfort available because of his own pain. Christ was unjustly accused, publicly shamed, horrendously beaten, horrifically crucified, and divinely forsaken on the cross. All comfort was removed from Christ so that we might be comforted—and be able to comfort one another. (p. 108)

Prayer Based on 2 Corinthians 1:3–7

God and Father of our Lord Jesus Christ, you are merciful. And you, Father, are the source of all comfort. You comfort us in all our troubles so that we can comfort others. When trouble comes, help us to remember and rest in your comfort so that we're prepared not to turn inward upon ourselves, but rather to comfort others with the same comfort you have given to us. Amen.

Group Discussion

Small groups reading *I Still Do* together can work through each of the reflection questions above. In addition, here is one more group discussion question for this chapter.

In the chapter I wrote, "God is so serious about helping you care for your spouse that he arranged some past affliction for you" (p. 106). Share with the group how God has comforted you through suffering and how this has prepared you to give comfort to your spouse.

DEFINING MOMENT #6:

The Moment You "Get" Mercy

> The quality of mercy is not strained;
> It droppeth as the gentle rain from heaven
> Upon the place beneath. It is twice blest;
> It blesseth him that gives and him that takes.
>
> William Shakespeare, *The Merchant of Venice*

If you want to help newlyweds have a long marriage, help them learn to forgive. If you've been married for any time at all, you discover that few things reveal the heart like sharing bathrooms and bank accounts. In a broken world, the silliest issues can ignite fireworks. Kimm and I had a conflict the other day because I felt like I'd waited too long for her. Truth to tell, I'm horribly impatient. And to round it out, Kimm doesn't live in a very time-conscious way. Throwing our two personalities together in a marriage has convinced me that the Trinity has a sense of humor. I imagine them laughing as Kimm and I explain to one another why our disposition toward or away from time-conscientiousness is superior.

Most of our married life is lived in monotonous moments. How a young couple is postured toward one another during the daily grind—that is, where each spouse's heart goes when they face their beloved's weakness and sin—determines whether or not the marriage is strong.

"Everyone says forgiveness is a lovely idea," C. S. Lewis observed, "until they have something to forgive."[1] In marriage you learn there is much to forgive and even more to be forgiven for. When two people learn to bring grace and forgiveness into the tedium of real life, they find their hearts slowly tenderized toward each other's frailty and fallenness. It's particularly true when a larger failure happens.

Stu and Linda met at church, fell in love, and soon eloped. Stu loved Linda, but he had secrets. For the last four years, Stu had been deeply entrenched in the worst kinds of pornography. It started simply as an intoxicating diversion, but he began to justify it as a legitimate stress-reliever. Stu was soon consumed by it. He'd get up in the middle of the night to pop on a site, he'd access his secret stash during work breaks, and sometimes he'd pull away at home to indulge his lust.

One night Linda stumbled across a site Stu had left open. Stu's explanation was unrehearsed, and Linda could tell within moments that he was lying. Linda felt defrauded, polluted, betrayed, and even frightened. She had no idea how deep this darkness had penetrated into Stu's soul. At first Stu felt caught but still victimized by Linda's intrusion on his computer. But eventually he saw that as incidental. He began to feel like he needed to seize this moment and come clean. Stu told Linda everything. Thankfully, his porn had not led him into adultery. But to Linda it felt like adultery. Lust is adultery of the heart (Matt. 5:27–30).

Stu saw Linda's pain, which only deepened his conviction. With sincere sorrow and genuine tears, Stu said, "Linda, I have lied to you, betrayed you, and concocted a secret life where looking at

1. C. S. Lewis, *Mere Christianity* (New York: HarperCollins, 2001), 115.

other women gave me pleasure. It's a sin before God and it's a betrayal toward you. Please, PLEASE forgive me!"

Perhaps the most painfully courageous part of forgiveness is that it involves absorbing the cost of a spouse's sin. The pain of being sinned against doesn't go away quickly. Words spoken, money lost, vows broken—these pains get stuck on repeat. For Linda, forgiveness meant she knew her husband had deceived her in dozens of ways. It also meant that she now had to compete, or at least felt as if she had to compete, against the airbrushed images of perfectly endowed women half her age.

Cost-absorbing forgiveness is rarely instantaneous. The words "I forgive you" are freely offered with a faith toward God, but they can betray the chaos within. Heartache and mental anguish can break into your mind unannounced. They creep up when you're down and can greet you the moment you wake.

Linda felt all of that. After all, to treat our spouse as their sin deserves—with anger, withdrawal, or emotional punishment—seems fairer, more equitable. But when you do this, you've forgotten just how much you've already been forgiven. You've forgotten the debt Christ paid for you. You were forgiven a great debt. Marriage often means doing the same.

Reading

Chapter 7 of *I Still Do*
Matthew 18:21–35
Colossians 3:12–14

Reflection Questions

Here is a selection of reflection questions and activities designed to fire your affections and get you thinking deeply about the truths presented in this chapter. Grab your Bible and a pen. Write out your answers and reflections and then share them with your spouse.

1. What do you think C. S. Lewis meant when he wrote, "Everyone says forgiveness is a lovely idea until they have something to forgive"? What are some of the things in us that make showing mercy so difficult?

2. How does Linda, who has clearly been sinned against, find a way to see beyond her pain to consider forgiving Stu? Where does the gospel offer her hope to take those first courageous steps?

3. Think about a time when you have absorbed the cost for another person's sin. If you are journaling, write out the story. If you are in a group and the person you are thinking about is not in the group, share the situation without mentioning any names. What truths enabled you to bear the cost of another's action? What did you learn from the experience?

---

4. When we consistently feel like we are getting less than we deserve in our marriage, how does the life and death of Jesus connect with our feelings and lead us to a different place?

Prayer Based on Colossians 3:12–14

Father, help us to truly comprehend what it means that you have poured out your mercy upon us by forgiving us of our sins—past, present and future! May our growing understanding of our forgiven sins make us more passionate to extend that same forgiveness to each other, beginning with our spouse. Help us to forgive those who have sinned against us as you also have forgiven us. Amen.

Group Discussion

Small groups reading *I Still Do* together can work through each of the reflection questions above. In addition, here is one more group discussion question for this chapter.

Forgiveness is costly because the debt incurred by someone else's sin does not just mysteriously evaporate. When we forgive, we often must accept the cost of bearing that burden. To truly forgive means we absorb the liability of what someone else owes. We don't retaliate; we don't strike back. We no longer hold them hostage in our heart until we can deliver them justice by our actions. But there are times when we must both forgive and yet still allow other people to bear the consequences of their sin (Num. 14:20–23). Discuss some situations in which consequences may be important to reclaiming and restoring a sinner.

CHAPTER

8

DEFINING MOMENT #7:

When You Discover Sex
Changes with Age

*Sex will never be pleasurable or durable when it's driven by
the demands of one instead of the enjoyment of two.*

I Still Do, p. 138

S ex is super, but it's also temporal. Even when we speak of
"lasting sex," we are talking only of this life. There is no
marriage in heaven (Matt. 22:30), so from the standpoint of Scripture, that means we won't be having sex. But sex, like marriage,
was never meant to be an end in itself. God would never dispose
of something so glorious if there weren't something better with
which to replace it. Sex was created as a foretaste of something
greater—the superior joy and delight we will experience being
with Jesus in the new heaven and new earth.

This truth—that marriage is temporary and meant as a sign
to point us to Jesus—may hit you in a couple of different ways.
Some of you may be saying, "Good. Sex was always filled with bag-
gage for us, and doing without it represents no great loss." Other
couples may be deeply disappointed. You'll miss experiencing one

another in such an intimate and enjoyable way. You might even ask, "How can God be glorified in heaven by denying us one of the few ecstasies we've experienced on earth?" I love the way C. S. Lewis answered this concern. Here's what he wrote in his book *Miracles*:

> I think our present outlook might be like that of a small boy, who, on being told that the sexual act was the highest bodily pleasure should immediately ask whether you ate chocolates at the same time. On receiving the answer "No," he might regard absence of chocolates as the chief characteristic of sexuality. In vain would you tell him that the reason why lovers in their carnal raptures don't bother about chocolates is that they have something better to think of. The boy knows chocolate: he does not know the positive thing that excludes it.
>
> We are in the same position. We know the sexual life; we do not know, except in glimpses, the other things which, in Heaven, will leave no room for it.[1]

My friends, the end of sex will be the beginning of something more glorious, something that exceeds the once-a-day demands of the seventy-year-old Starbucks customer (remember him from the book?), something better than you could possibly imagine. Pleasure in a sin-saturated world is always muted by our fallenness. But a day is coming when we will slip the bonds of brokenness to experience pleasure in a wholly pure and unobstructed way. An orgasm on earth won't begin to compare to the delight of being in the presence of the divine dance between the persons of the Trinity. There is greater joy in joining in eternal communion with God. That's the end for which we have been created.

So enjoy sex while you have it. But do so remembering that the best is yet to come!

1. C. S. Lewis, *Miracles* (New York: Collier Books, 1960), 159–60.

Reading

Chapter 8 of *I Still Do*
Song of Solomon 1:1–2:1
Matthew 22:23–33

Reflection Questions

Here is a selection of reflection questions and activities modeled after the Wise Talk sections found in chapter 8 of *I Still Do*. The goal of these questions is to get you thinking deeply about the truths presented in this chapter. Grab your Bible and a pen. Write out your answers and reflections and then share them with your spouse.

1. The past has a powerful impact on how we think about sex in the present. Can you identify any positive ways the past has shaped how you think about sex? God often surprises us with hidden delights in the bedroom. Can you describe for your spouse a specific way God has surprised you? Let's also flip it over. Are there any ways the past has obscured the place of healthy sexuality? What bad fruit can you locate? Don't be afraid to stare brokenness in the face. God is bigger, and grace rushes at us when we open our soul in such intimate ways. Go to God in prayer together. He is there, poised to bless your humble steps toward him (James 4:6).

2. There is no "normal" sex life. Normal can't be prescribed. It must be defined through careful conversation. Talk together about what kind of rhythm would best serve your marriage in this season. Talk can only be wise when it happens, so don't allow the delicacy of this topic to go unaddressed. Invite each other to honestly comment on your frequency dial. Is it set at the right level? Why or why not? Don't accuse. Ask questions and listen to your spouse's response. Remember, sex is a conversation topic God has already initiated with us in his Word. Move in with confidence, then, believing that God wants to bless your attempts to understand and love each other in better ways.

3. Think about the things grace says to us that I outlined in the chapter:

   "My vision of handsome or beautiful is my spouse."

   "The past should stay there."

   "I will not define you by your worst moments."

   Which one of these truths that grace speaks seems most relevant to your marriage? Ask your spouse to answer the same question and listen to their response. How do you respond to realities about your sex life that your spouse sees but you don't? Find the grace that comes from responding to your spouse in humility (James 4:6).

_____

_____

_____

_____

Prayer Based on Matthew 22:23–33

Father, thank you for giving us the gift of sex. We delight in it now, but help us not to make it an ultimate thing. Help us to see the better glory of eternal marriage with you. Help us to know that an orgasm on earth won't begin to compare to the delight of being in your presence. Strengthen us in hope for eternal communion so that we might extend greater grace to one another here. Amen.

Group Discussion

The questions above are more intimate than in other chapters of this workbook. They are designed more for discussion between a husband and wife. Small groups reading *I Still Do* may simply discuss what key truths from the chapter or from the discussion questions above were most impactful. In addition, here is one more group discussion question for this chapter.

In the chapter I told the story of a seventy-year-old Starbucks patron who demanded sex once each day. What would you say if you were the counselor sitting with him in Starbucks? How would your counsel change if the man were younger, perhaps in his thirties, forties, fifties, or sixties? How would your counsel stay the same?

ENDING T♥GETHER

DEFINING MOMENT #8:

When Dreams Disappoint

> Everyone marries with a dream. Our outlook is profoundly shaped by what we expect to see. And many of us entered wedlock so focused on our dreams that we missed some gorilla-like realities.
>
> *I Still Do*, p. 154

These days, the network ratings for wedding shows are spiking upward. I'm reluctant to list the top ten, since the names and ranking will change by the time this study guide goes to print. But whatever the most popular hit, the wedding shows are a testimony to some deeply held cultural convictions now woven into our collective psyche. Here's one of the clearest: *The wedding, not the life that follows, is what we prepare for.* You may not have heard it described quite that way, but you've probably heard one of these catchphrases:

- "This is the biggest day of the bride's life!"
- "Say yes to the most awesome dress!"
- "Spare no expense on the ceremony or reception."

- "Your wedding must be unique and distinct from every other wedding in the history of the world."
- "The rest of your life will be determined by this event!"

Some of this is understandable. It's not defiant ignorance or gross negligence. It's just really hard to see any terrain that lies beyond the mountain of "I do." Being engaged is like walking through an amusement park with fogged-up glasses. Looking ahead may be fuzzy, but who cares? There's a buzz of excitement and you're having fun! And the elusive wait, the "I-can't-believe-it's-happening-to-me" . . . well, it's actually happening to you. The wedding is almost here.

Then the day arrives! The ceremony, the family, the pomp, the ritual. Everyone's excited—it all feels surreal. And let's be honest. Filling the anticipation are the caged sexual desires of a new husband and wife about to roam free in the highlands of marriage. When the ceremony officiant says "I now pronounce you man and wife," newlyweds hear "Have at it!"

The emotion, stress, and sexual anticipation of wedding prep supercharges the day with enormous significance. So the well-meaning intent of premarital counseling, even when it's done well, is largely lost. Doing marriage counseling while planning a wedding is akin to buying a house sight unseen. You see a three-bedroom, mid-century, Craftsman-style home online. It's a solid house in a good neighborhood. It all seems so perfect! You may do some research on the broker's website and consult people you trust and respect, but life is just too crazy to do a walk-through. So you make the purchase. Then, when you get the keys and begin to unload boxes, reality sets in. Only in the days following is the full cost understood.

Think about what really happens when a couple stands at the altar and says "I do" in the presence of those who love them. Most often, those two people arrive with practiced expectations.

They expect overwhelming emotional benefits from this marriage. They're looking for fulfillment of their needs and an emotional "You complete me!" experience of marriage. As they recite their vows, a cluster of unspoken beliefs and hopes musters in the hidden vaults of their hearts. Locked away for now are deep desires, anticipations, dreams, and unmet needs. They pulse with hope of how the nuptials will fill the empty voids they represent. But what happens when our dreams for marriage disappoint?

Reading

Chapter 9 of *I Still Do*
Proverbs 13:12; 17:17
John 15:12–17
James 4:1–10

Reflection Questions

Here is a selection of reflection questions and activities designed to fire your affections and get you thinking deeply about the truths presented in this chapter. Grab your Bible and a pen. Write out your answers and reflections and then share them with your spouse.

1. When couples enter into marriage, they dream about how love will keep them together through the years. And it can. But whether or not love keeps us together depends largely on how we define love. How do you define love? Was your definition of love challenged by the reading in the chapter? Why or why not?

_____

_____

_____

_____

_____

_____

2. Love involves both losing ("Burn the ships!") and gaining (promise-centered endurance, being known, godliness). Describe in your journal some of the things that you've gained and lost in love.

_____

_____

_____

_____

_____

3. In the corresponding chapter I wrote about how your marital friendship must be your highest priority next to your friendship with Jesus. Our friendship with our spouse fans the flames of marital romance and is one of the most important motivators for enduring faithfulness. Take the marriage friendship quiz below and talk over the results with your spouse. How is your marital friendship doing?

_____

_____

_____

_____

_____

_____

IS YOUR MARITAL FRIENDSHIP PRIMED FOR ROMANCE AND ENDURANCE?

The following quiz, adapted from John M. Gottman and Nan Silver, *The Seven Principles for Making Marriage Work: A Practical Guide from the Country's Foremost Relationship Expert*, rev. ed. (New York: Harmony, 2015), 90–91, will give you a good sense of how your marriage friendship is doing.

Circle T for true or F for false.

1. **T F** We enjoy doing small activities together like washing the dishes or watching TV.
2. **T F** I enjoy spending my free time with my spouse. We have a good time together.
3. **T F** At the end of the day, my spouse is glad to see me.
4. **T F** I enjoy discussing things with my spouse.
5. **T F** My spouse is one of my best friends.
6. **T F** We enjoy our times of prayer and devotions together.
7. **T F** We just love talking to each other.
8. **T F** When we go out together, the time goes very quickly.
9. **T F** We always have a lot to say to each other.
10. **T F** My spouse tells me when he or she has had a bad day.
11. **T F** We tend to share the same basic values.
12. **T F** We like to spend time together in similar ways.
13. **T F** We have many of the same dreams and goals.
14. **T F** We have common interests. We like to do a lot of the same things.
15. **T F** Even though our interests are somewhat different, I enjoy my spouse's interests.

Scoring: Give yourself one point for each true answer. If your score is below 9, your marital friendship could demand some attention.

Friendship becomes a dream deferred if we don't fight to protect it. "Hope deferred makes the heart sick, but a desire fulfilled is a tree of life" (Prov. 13:12). Prioritizing friendship means your spouse is your first earthly priority. And yes, this means the antiquated face-to-face variety of friendship where sitting, looking, sharing, and experiencing each other is not replaced by merely functional modes of communication.

Prayer Based on Psalm 30:11–12

Father, you are the One who promises to take even what we perceive as losses and griefs and make them into something beautiful. As the psalmist says:

> *You have turned for me my mourning into dancing;*
> *you have loosed my sackcloth*
> *and clothed me with gladness,*
> *that my glory may sing your praise and not be silent.*
> *O Lord my God, I will give thanks to you forever!*
> *Amen.*

Group Discussion

Small groups reading *I Still Do* together can work through each of the reflection questions above. In addition, here is one more group activity for this chapter.

Consider the following internal dialogue of a couple at the altar, which I've adapted for this study guide from Larry Crabb Jr., *The Marriage Builder* (Grand Rapids: Zondervan, 1982), 31.

Groom: I need to feel significant, and I expect you, my new wife, to affirm me by following my leadership closely, whether it makes sense to you or not. I need to be respected, regardless of how I behave. It seems to me like God wants you to fully support me, even when you see me fallen, flawed, or failing. As my helpmate, your loyalty toward me should be unwavering enthusiasm and support in keeping with the reality that I'm now the most important man in the world for you. My goal in loving you is to love myself more, because I sometimes deal with feelings of inferiority and shame. An arrangement in which you are commanded by God to submit to me seems very timely and will support me, I suspect, in my journey to better love myself. So, with this ring, I kiss my unmet needs goodbye.

Bride: I have never felt understood in the way I need. Up to this day, no one has loved me as deeply as my nature requires. But God has now embedded you, my new husband, in my life to love me like Christ loves the church. This means you will always put me first, sacrifice continuously for me, live heedless of your own desires, and faithfully overlook my weaknesses. I expect unconditional love even when I'm angry. I expect patient consideration whether or not I'm reciprocating with the same. I expect a persistent and compassionate sensitivity to my emotional ups and downs. So, with this ring, I give you my needs. Don't let me down.

Perhaps I've exaggerated these internal conversations, but they illustrate an undeniable point. Most couples get married with expectations that their spouse exists—or, in more spiritual parlance, "has been given by God"—to meet their unmet needs. If we could have eavesdropped on your subconscious when you stood at the altar, what might we have heard? How have your expectations been challenged and changed during the course of your marriage?

DEFINING MOMENT #9:

When the Kids Leave

It's rare for a young couple to start a new family with mature humility.

I Still Do, p. 176

D o you remember what your marriage preparation was like? In chapter 1 of this study guide, I told the story of what it was like for me and Kimm. We had one premarital session before our wedding, and it was focused almost exclusively upon sex. There was no discussion about the complications of sex. Rather, we were told, "You need to talk about it." A well-meaning counselor handed us a crate of cassette tapes that we promptly lost in the trunk of my car—at least until the counselor asked for them back several months after our wedding.

Whatever our experience, we know intuitively that couples need to be prepared *before* marriage.

But did you know that there's another kind of preparation that's necessary *within* marriage? It's preparation of a variety that determines how well you will live and love in your later years. Let's call it "empty-nest training." Most couples give this kind of training about as much attention as Kimm and I gave our pre-marital counseling.

Empty-nest training involves . . .

- accepting the way authority changes
- avoiding the traps of becoming either demanding parents or needy parents in your relationships with your adult children
- anticipating the emotional impact around your kids' departure
- foreseeing an understandable distance now that the kids have left
- investing in your own marriage
- considering meaningful ways that you can serve your adult children

Reading

Chapter 10 of *I Still Do*
Daniel 2
John 13:1–17

Reflection Questions

Here is a selection of reflection questions and activities designed to fire your affections and get you thinking deeply about the truths presented in this chapter. Grab your Bible and a pen.

1. In the chapter I wrote, "Every family is its own civiliza-tion, complete with culture, dialect, and treasured arti-facts" (p. 172). What things about your family culture could seem foreign to a new son- or daughter-in-law?

_____

_____

_____

_____

_____

2. As our kids grow older, our authority begins to shift. C. S. Lewis foresaw this shifting role:

> The proper aim of giving is to put the recipient in a state where he no longer needs our gift. We feed children in order that they may soon be able to feed themselves; we teach them in order that they may soon not need our teaching. Thus, a heavy task is laid upon this Gift-love. It must work towards its own abdication. We must aim at making ourselves super-fluous. The hour when we can say "They need me no longer" should be our reward.[1]

Consider this quote, write reflections in your journal, and share them with your spouse.

_____

_____

_____

_____

_____

_____

1. C. S. Lewis, *The Four Loves* (New York: Harcourt, Brace and Company, 1960), 76.

3. In the chapter I wrote, "Pay careful attention to what makes you angry, because what incites your wrath reveals your heart" (p. 177). As your kids have gotten older, when have you found yourself getting most angry with them? What is it that makes you angry? Take time to reflect on this and confess it to your spouse.

4. The healthiest kind of family system is one where the parents hold up a mirror for their kids. Needy parents, by contrast, attempt to fulfill their own desires through their kids. Reflect back on your last conversation with your son or daughter. Were you more concerned with reflecting back their emotions or with having them affirm your thoughts and feelings?

Prayer Based on Philippians 2:5–11

Father, you show us what it looks like to be the ultimate parent—always giving support rather than needing it. Jesus, you show us how to give away authority and respect rather

*than cling to them. You did not consider equality with God—
and the honor and respect that came with that position—as
something to use to your advantage, but instead you emptied
yourself and took the form of a servant. Help me to do the
same as I serve my children. Amen.*

Group Discussion

Small groups reading *I Still Do* together can work through each
of the reflection questions above. In addition, here is one more
group activity for this chapter.

Sweet Honey in the Rock, an African American a capella ensemble,
adapted a poem by Khalil Gibran titled "On Children." If you've
ever watched your kid say "I do" and then kissed them good-bye,
the words of this song toll like an old bell within your soul:[2]

> Your children are not your children.
> They are the sons and daughters of Life's longing for
>   itself.
> They come through you but not from you,
> And though they are with you yet they belong not to you.

The song goes on to describe how we give our kids affection,
shelter, and direction, but we can't control what they take, "for
they have thoughts of their own." We love our kids, but we can't
determine their futures. Consider this quote and share your reflections with the group.

2. Sweet Honey in the Rock, "On Children," *Breaths*, track 12 (Flying Fish,
1988), compact disc.

11

DEFINING MOMENT #10:

When You Learn Closure Is Overrated

We don't find peace by getting ultimate answers. We find peace only by clinging to a good God in the midst of perplexing pain.

I Still Do, p. 192

Daddy's a jackass!" Sharon blurted it out before she even knew what she was saying. The kids froze, staring at Sharon, their eyes wide and astonishment pasted across their faces. "That's right," Sharon thought. "It's time they knew." Donnie, her husband for over a decade, had met a younger woman two years earlier, and they now shared an apartment four blocks over so that Donnie could remain meaningfully involved with the kids. Meaningful involvement in his marriage had ended many years back. Donnie just moved on. It's what Donnie always did.

Sharon had just heard from a neighbor that Donnie and his girlfriend were soon to be Donnie and his second wife.

Sharon seethed. This was not her dream; this was not the way the marriage story was supposed to be written. Sharon, after all, had fought hard for her marriage. While they were still together, Sharon prayed, pursued counseling, and sought to be long-suffering with Donnie's drifts. She was confident he would come around, certain that her steadfast love and forbearing heart would penetrate the discontent that corrupted Donnie's happiness. But nothing worked. Donnie just got worse. Eventually he just left.

Sharon did everything right and it all went wrong. And now Donnie was getting remarried.

"It feels so unjust." Sharon sighed. "All of my work to save this marriage was *wasted*. And all I have to show for it is this giant, gaping wound in my heart." Sharon was not exaggerating her reality. Donnie showed no signs of being sorry for what he had done. In fact, in his moral universe, he felt entirely justified.

Now Sharon stares in the mirror. Looking back is someone who is having difficulty understanding why her faithfulness bore so little fruit. What's more, there's no closure in sight, no apologies on the horizon. Only the unsettling reality that life is hard, people are inconsistent, and being a Christian does not mean that sinful choices always get resolved.

Sharon whispers to her reflection, "I can't believe this is your life."

We are encountering Sharon in the middle of her story. We don't know the ways God will use these circumstances to reveal himself to Sharon or work through these painful experiences to achieve her good. But the story illustrates an important point that must be understood to achieve a resilient marriage.

Earth is not heaven. Sometimes it feels like hell. Our stories don't always seem to end well. People we love display vast inconsistencies between what they say and what they do. Hard situations don't resolve in the way they should. Sometimes things get worse. If we live expecting heaven, it's not long before we're crashing to earth.

This broken world is inherently open-ended. It's aimed for heaven. It even prepares us for heaven. But it's not heaven. What makes marriage crazy, or people crazy in marriage, is expecting the stuff of heaven—perfection, unending consistency, and complete closure—when we inhabit a world fragmented by sin.

It's human to be taken captive by expectations—to long for a better spouse or crave the closure that allows us to move on. In this life, however, we must live in a way that desires these things but does not *need* them in order to be at peace. Our peace is drawn from the completed work of Jesus Christ. Because of the injustice done to him, we can enjoy peace.

The cross represents closure on the most important yet un-resolved and open-ended matter in the universe—our rebellion against the almighty God. When Jesus died in our place, he absorbed the penalty that we deserved and gave us his forgiveness. This means that there may be much about my life or marriage that remains unresolved, but we possess closure on what matters most. Because of the closure God gives, we can enjoy peace, even when our whole world seems to be collapsing inward.

Reading

Chapter 11 of *I Still Do*
2 Timothy 3:1–4:18
Hebrews 11

Reflection Questions

Here is a selection of reflection questions and activities designed to fire your affections and get you thinking deeply about the truths presented in this chapter. Grab your Bible and a pen.

1. What makes marriage crazy—or people crazy in marriage—is expecting consistency and resolution when you inhabit a place fragmented by sin. A broken world is inherently open-ended. In what ways have you expected the ideal of perfect closure in your marriage?

_____

_____

_____

_____

2. We need a faith that is rooted in God's faithfulness. Does your understanding of God's activity and providence leave room for open-ended things in this life? Or do your experiences simply provide an excuse for you to become bitter and cynical, living life as if you've been defrauded by God?

_____

_____

_____

_____

3. Are you aware of any particular unmet expectations, losses, or failures that you have not sufficiently grieved? How are you responding to them? Are you protecting yourself from disappointment and pain at all costs? Or are you believing that the reconciliation you most need has already been won for us in Christ, even when you can't see it in your circumstances?

_____

_____

_____

_____

_____

Prayer Based on 2 Timothy 4:16–18

Father, even if no one else supports me, help me to know your presence at my side, giving me strength. Even if everyone deserts me, do not hold it against them. Rather, when my pain is open-ended and unresolved, may it be used as a testimony to help others. Lord, I know you will bring me safely to your heavenly kingdom, and there you finally will bring closure. Glory and honor be to you, Lord, forever and ever. Amen.

Group Discussion

Small groups reading *I Still Do* together can work through each of the reflection questions above. In addition, here is one more group activity for this chapter.

Reflect on how the good news of what Christ has done in the *past* as well as what he promises to do in the *future* speaks to your lack of closure. Write out specific ways Christ's work and Christ's promises minister to you in the midst of your open-ended circumstances.

Christ's Work in the Past. When a lack of resolution darkens the present, we can first go back to what Christ accomplished on Golgotha and remember "It is finished!" Sweet closure has been achieved. Our lives certainly are not wrapped up with tiny bows. There are areas where, like Paul, our relational world remains painfully open-ended. Maybe it's a former spouse, an old friend, even someone in the family. We've tried, but we just aren't reconciled in the way we desire.

It's so good to remember that, because of Christ, you already possess the reconciliation that matters most. As a believer you wake up every morning with your most important relationship intact. By loving you enough to die for your sins, Christ has met your deepest need. How does what Christ has done for you in the past comfort you today?

Christ's Promises for the Future. But there's more good news. Our hope doesn't simply remain tucked away in the past. Lift your eyes to see a future coming! The future carries the closure that presently eludes you. The anticipation of a new heaven and new earth reminds us that unresolved conflicts, marriage challenges, betrayal, injustice, and broken relationships are temporary pains. Resolution is speeding toward you with the passing of every moment of every day. People who may cross the street to avoid the awkwardness of greeting you will soon weep for joy at the sight of you in the world to come. Every bad seed with a heart bent toward evil will be either converted or condemned. The pleasure of unending joy will replace the pain of unresolved questions.

Only a certain future like this can temper our momentary grievances. How does what Christ has promised to do for you in the future comfort you today?

Do you find more comfort from looking to the past or by looking toward the future?

12

When Grace Conquers Your Wasted Moments: *The Death of Ivan Ilych*

> What can be done for a man whose dying breaths are haunted by wasted relationships, a wasted marriage, and a wasted life?
>
> *I Still Do*, p. 207

For the first ten defining moments in *I Still Do*, I provided summary charts at the end of each chapter. Here is a summary chart for the final defining moment—death. As life's close nears, you may face disappointments over missed opportunities in your marriage. Consider the chart below and take a few moments to consider how you will respond.

Defining Moment #11:
The Wasted Moments

	The Moment	Our Response
The Decision for Truth	Will I indulge selfish, propped-up delusions in public that are inconsistent with my private questions and fears?	*Or* will I live a life of self-examination?
The Cost Required	Will I compare myself to others in a manner that convinces me that they are the problem and that I'm entitled to more?	*Or* will I own and confess my thousands of self-obsessed acts and omissions before a holy God?
The God-Exalting Opportunity	Will I isolate myself and immediately give in to self-pity and despair when suffering or pain arrives?	*Or* will I honor God by anticipating suffering and seek to glorify him when it inevitably comes?
The Way It Grows the Soul	Will I recognize that the self-indulgent life is defined by either performance or suffering?	*Or* will I acknowledge now that Christ's victory redefines us and delivers us from the sting of sin and death into confidence, joy, and hope?
The Way It Sets Our Destination	Will I come to terms with the reality that the road to hell is paved with people who, on the surface, seem to have ordinary lives—and yet when you dig below, you discover bad motives and a myriad of terrible choices?	*Or*, when I have a defining moment and see a wasted opportunity, will I remember that grace appears at the unforgiving bottom of waste? Will I remember that it saves even the worst of sinners?

Reading

Chapter 12 of *I Still Do*
Matthew 20:1–16
Luke 23:32–43
Jude 24–25

Reflection Questions

Here is a selection of reflection questions and activities designed to fire your affections and get you thinking deeply about the truths presented in this chapter. Grab your Bible and a pen.

1. In the chapter I wrote, "Ivan is not merely a man; he is a symbol of life lived without God—the epic consequence of a distracted existence" (p. 202). What comforts and distractions move your gaze away from God's purposes in your life?

2. In his passing hour, Ivan becomes aware of a lifetime of regrets. What regrets and wasted moments are you aware of in your life? List them out in your journal and later share them with your spouse.

3. When we first become aware of regrets, our tendency is to try and excuse ourselves. In the chapter I wrote, "Buried deeply in us all is a defense attorney who denies our

culpability and desperately searches for evidence to rationalize thousands of self-obsessed acts and omissions" (p. 206). How do you try to rationalize your failures? What are the excuses you gravitate toward?

_____

_____

_____

_____

_____

4. Undeserved grace for a wasted life shouldn't merely stir your gratitude; it should fire your ambition to change. Grace stands ready to forgive your past, and in the chapter I talked about three practical ways that it stands ready to reorient your perspective.

Consider each one:

Grace contends for our holiness. Do you see your spouse as God's gift to help you change? How could adopting that perspective help your relationship?

_____

_____

_____

_____

Grace intercepts our isolation and moves us to confession. Are there persistent sins that you have been hiding from God and your spouse? Grace covers all these sins.

Bring them to the light. Confess them to God and your spouse today.

_____

_____

_____

_____

_____

Grace wins so we can put aside our performance. How does remembering Christ's performance for you minister to you in the midst of your regrets? How can it free you from guilt?

_____

_____

_____

_____

_____

Prayer Based on Jude 24–25

Because grace wins, friends, you can face your final moments with confidence and hope. Pray this closing prayer of praise.

Now to him who is able to keep you from stumbling and to present you blameless before the presence of his glory with great joy, to the only God, our Savior, through Jesus Christ our Lord, be glory, majesty, dominion, and authority, before all time and now and forever. Amen.

Group Discussion

Small groups reading *I Still Do* together can work through each of the reflection questions above. In addition, here is one more group activity for this chapter.

Review Matthew 20:1–16. Do you identify with the guys in the story who worked all day? Are you tempted to think that the master in this parable is unfair and that those who worked all day deserved more than was promised? Is there a part of you that begrudges those who seem to deserve less than you when they receive mercy?

God's generosity toward some is not his injustice toward others. Why is God's mercy toward the undeserving such good news? Discuss this as a group.

Dave Harvey (DMin, Westminster Theological Seminary) serves as the president of Great Commission Collective, a church planting ministry in the US, Canada, and abroad. Dave founded AmI Called.com, pastored for thirty-three years, serves on the board of CCEF, and travels widely across networks and denominations as a popular conference speaker. He is the author of the bestselling *When Sinners Say "I Do,"* as well as *Am I Called?* and *Rescuing Ambition*, and a coauthor of *Letting Go: Rugged Love for Wayward Souls*. He and his wife, Kimm, have four kids and four grandchildren and live in southwest Florida. For videos, articles, or to book an event, visit www.revdaveharvey.com.

A Lasting Marriage Is Built
ONE DEFINING MOMENT
at a Time

Learn to recognize the life-defining moments of a post-newlywed marriage so you can take a proactive, godly approach to resolving conflicts, hold each other up as change inevitably happens, and ensure your marriage not only survives but thrives.

Connect with
DAVE!

To discover more content from Dave Harvey and
find more resources for marriage and ministry, visit

RevDaveHarvey.com

  @RevDaveHarvey